How to Save Money On Groceries Without Coupons

35 Money-Saving Ideas to Eat Better for Less

Madeleine Mayfair

How to Save Money on Groceries Without Coupons
© 2018 Madeleine Mayfair

The contents of this book are for informational purposes only and do not constitute professional advice.

Cover design © 2018 Madeleine Mayfair

ISBN-13: 978-1983585920
ISBN-10: 1983585920

Are you tired of overspending on everyday items? Want to eat better for less? And do it all without clipping coupons? Then this is the book for you! Establish a budget and stay on track with 35 easy-to-implement ideas. Just a few easy tweaks to your regular shopping habits could save you cash every month, and help you get the most out of your hard-earned money! Find out how with How to Save Money on Groceries Without Coupons: 35 Money-Saving Ideas to Eat Better for Less!

HOW TO SAVE MONEY ON GROCERIES WITHOUT COUPONS

INTRODUCTION

Who wants to save money on groceries without using coupons?

I do! I do!

By why no coupons? What's wrong with coupons?

Nothing at all! Coupons are great. I used to be a coupon fanatic—well, maybe not as much of a fanatic as the people you see on TV, but I loved coupons a whole lot. In the early 2000s, I even belonged to a "coupon train" which was established by a dozen or so members of a money-saving forum I belonged to.

Coupon train? What's that?

Our coupon train was useful and fun. The first member kicked things off by filling an envelope with manufacturers' coupons she wouldn't be using. She'd then post that envelope to the next person, geographically, who would take out the coupons she would use and replace those with coupons she'd collected that she wouldn't be using.

For instance, I used to accumulate a lot of coupons for diapers and baby products. I'm not a parent, but a lot of the other coupon train members were. Coupons that weren't useful for me proved essential for them. We'd share the wealth and usually include a few cutesy items like stickers, just for fun.

So if coupons are so great, why'd you stop using them?

It's kind of a sad story. One time I was at the register in a supermarket and the cashier had a question about a "free product" coupon. She'd called her manager to ask him if she was okay to accept it.

The man behind me in line became very belligerent while waiting for the manager. He started screaming and swearing, mostly at me. When his hostility didn't speed things up, he rammed me viciously with his shopping cart.

The cashier was clearly too afraid of the customer to do anything. When the manager arrived I told him what had just happened, but there were no repercussions for the man who had physically assaulted me.

After that, I noticed myself feeling nervous every time I went to pull out a coupon. I guess a part of me equated coupons with the assault. Even if there hadn't been a physical component to that encounter, the abusive customer's screaming and shouting still would have echoed in my mind.

Slowly, I stopped using coupons altogether. For years I told myself I'd simply outgrown my interest in coupons. But now, looking back, I realize it was that incident of verbal abuse and physical assault that led me off the couponing path.

That was a downer!

I know! I'm sorry! I certainly hope you've never encountered abuse in line at the grocery store. I just wanted to give you an idea of why I've designed a money-saving plan that doesn't involve coupons. If you want to include coupons in your plan, that's great! You're going to save even more of your hard-earned money!

Happy Savings,
Your friend Maddie

THE ABSOLUTE BASICS

In the Long Term Planning section of this book, you'll find a great list of in-depth ideas to help you save money on groceries. Some are probably ideas you've already had. Some might be ideas you've already implemented. But I hope you'll be inspired to try out a few new practices.

Before we get to long-term planning, here are a few rules you should know so you can choose when to break them.

If you're brand-spanking-new to saving money on groceries, here's what you need to know:

1. Read grocery flyers before you leave the house.

Maybe you receive paper copies of flyers from local grocery stores delivered right to your house.

Sometimes I do, sometimes I don't. I'm not sure why. But luckily, flyers for just about every major store in the vicinity are available online. In fact, many stores' websites make upcoming flyers available in advance so you can decide whether holding off on buying this or that will save you big.

2. Make a list of what you need and see how that corresponds with what's on sale.

I used to work with a guy who had a funny Friday night routine with his wife. They received the local grocery flyers Friday afternoon. When his wife got home from work, she sat at the kitchen table, read the flyers, and made a list of things she thought they should buy. When my co-worker got home, it was his turn. He took the grocery flyers into "the reading room" and compiled his list on "the throne." After that, they sat together on the couch, watched TV, and discussed what was on their individual lists, ultimately compiling a final grocery list for the week. I thought it was adorable how their Friday night routine revolved around groceries.

3. When you go to the store, stick to your list.

This is the rule you'll break most often. At least, it's the rule I break most often. The key to saving money is learning when breaking this rule will benefit you and when it'll just break the bank.

Those are the basics. Simple, right? Now let's move on to long-term planning!

LONG-TERM PLANNING

Now we're getting to the meat of the book: ideas to help you save money without starving. In fact, a lot of these ideas will actually help you to eat better while spending less. That way, you get the best of both worlds!

1

CREATE A WEEKLY FOOD BUDGET AND STICK TO IT.

Budgeting! One of my favourite words! May not be to everyone's taste, but it's important to determine how much money you can reasonably afford to spend on food before you start spending.

And you know what? It might take a few months to figure out what's actually feasible.

If you have big-ticket items on your grocery list (like diapers, meal replacements, etc.) they might not come up every week. My biggest big-ticket item is cat food. My lucky cats eat better than I do! I don't skimp on their kibble, but I also don't buy it every week. Cat food only makes its way on to my list about once a month, but it costs my entire week's food budget so I need to plan ahead.

Planning ahead means you won't get caught short with nothing in the fridge!

2

BUDGET TROUBLES?
CASH COULD BE THE ANSWER.

So you've created a reasonable budget but you can't seem to stick to it. What now?

If you find you have trouble sticking to a food budget you should rightly be able to handle and willpower is an issue, opt for cash, not cards.

It's way easier to go over budget when money is an intangible substance. That's why we end up spending more if we're paying with a card. If you can see the cash and hold it in your hands, it means more to you. You won't want to spend it so easily. Plus, when it's gone, it's gone!

3

TAKE ADVANTAGE OF LOYALTY POINTS PROGRAMS FOR FREE GROCERIES.

These days, many supermarkets have their own in-house loyalty programs. That, or they're affiliated with larger programs or points cards.

Do a little investigating. Figure out where you're going to earn the most points, and how to earn them. Remember that, if the only way to earn points is by purchasing high-priced items you don't need, this is not where you want to focus your attention.

I do most of my shopping at a supermarket chain where I have a points card. Not just that, but I have a credit card that's affiliated with the points program, so every dollar I spend on anything anywhere earns me points I can spend in-store.

Every week, the points program sends me an email and when I click the link, I see items that, when purchased, will earn me bonus points. The system's algorithms are very clever. They know what I've purchased in the past and what I'm inclined to purchase again.

I don't buy anything I don't need just to capitalize on the points, but if they happen to offer me $4 in points when I buy my usual kitty litter (which I ALWAYS need), I'm all over that!

4

KNOW WHAT YOU'VE GOT.

Take a look through your fridge and cupboards before you leave for the shop. Make a mental note of what you already have on hand. This will help you to avoid buying yet another tub of mayonnaise when you've already got three at home.

5

AVOID THE URGE TO GO OVERBOARD.

There's a difference between stocking up and buying way more food than you're ever going to eat. Speaking as someone who was raised by a food hoarder, I've seen what happens when a person buys more than they need. It takes a psychological toll.

I get it. Cereal's on sale. You think, gee, it might never this cheap again. But please, I'm begging you, don't go crazy. Trust me, it's a slippery slope. Buy a little too much one week, a little too much the next, and soon enough you've got an entire room in your basement devoted to storing expired boxes of cereal. It can happen.

6

AVOID THE URGE TO BUY STUFF YOU'RE NEVER GOING TO EAT JUST BECAUSE IT'S ON SALE.

Has this ever happened to you? You're in the store, you come across a great sale item. You've never tried this product before, but it's such a great deal that you buy ten! You get it home. You give it a try. Yuck! You've never tasted anything so disgusting in all your life! Now you've just spent your hard-earned money on food you're never going to eat.

What a waste.

7

DON'T LET LOSS-LEADERS LEAD
TO A LOSS!

There's a supermarket near me that often has amazing deals on toilet paper.

Toilet paper is something pretty much every human is going to buy, unless you steal it from your office or use nothing but napkins from McDonalds (please don't do either of those things!), so supermarkets know they can get you in the door by offering it at a super-low price.

Works on me. All the time!

In fact, it works on most of us. Who wouldn't want to pay next to nothing for a product that goes right down the drain?

But here's the trap supermarkets count on: they know that, if they can get you through the door by offering something everybody needs at a low price, chances are you're going to pick up a few other items while you're there.

Most people are super-busy. We've got tons to do. If you know you need fruit and cheese and you're already at the store for toilet paper, you're probably going to buy your fruit and cheese while you're there, even if they cost a little more than you'd normally pay.

Once you're aware of the ways in which stores manipulate your purchase behaviour, at least you can be mindful of whether or not you want to fall into the traps they set.

8

KEEP AN EYE ON THE REGISTER.

Everybody makes mistakes, and computers are people too! Well, no they're not, but items very often scan at the wrong price. You want to catch those mistakes or you risk paying way too much for your groceries.

Depending on where you live, you might even get the product for free or at a discount if it scans wrong. Look into laws and store policies in your jurisdiction—I've received a bag of cat food for free when I mentioned to the cashier that it had scanned at $18.99 but the sign on the shelf said $17.99.

The cashier told me it was their store policy that, if an item scanned at the wrong price, the customer got that item free. I had no idea!

9

SHOP WHERE YOU CAN GET THE BEST DEALS

This seems like obvious advice, but it's worth mentioning.

It's also worth tossing a couple caveats into the mix. Because what if you live in a neighbourhood where everything is just... expensive?

There are a lot of pros and cons that go into choosing your supermarket, as you'll see in the following point.

TAKE TIME AND TRANSPORTATION INTO ACCOUNT WHEN CHOOSING WHERE TO SHOP

I live in a crowded urban centre where retail rents are very high. That means the supermarkets near my apartment are tiny and the food prices are out of this world.

If I were to shop in the suburbs, I would pay less for my food, but I'd also have to get there and back. I don't drive, so that means a bus ride with my groceries.

Are you a thrill-seeker by nature? You enjoy a good challenge? Try riding public transit with a week's worth of groceries. Some people do it all the time, and they are my heroes.

You run into the same situation if you live in a remote location. I realized this while visiting a friend who lives in a very small town. There was only one supermarket nearby, and the food prices there were exactly what I was used to in the downtown core of a big city.

My friend could save money by driving to a larger town that had a variety of bigger supermarkets, but then she had to take into account gas money plus the time out of her day it took to make that long drive there and back.

No matter where you live, it's worth taking into account gas money, transportation costs, distance, and the value of your time when considering the best place to shop.

11

GROW YOUR OWN FOOD.

No matter who you are or where you live, it is possible to grow a certain amount of food yourself. Heck, you can sprout alfalfa in your kitchen!

If you've got lots of outdoor space on your property, like a big backyard for instance, you're well-positioned to become the world's greatest gardener.

But maybe you're thinking "I live in an apartment. How am I supposed to grow food?"

Well, I live in an apartment too. I have a balcony that only gets a sliver of sunshine around 7 at night. By all rights, I shouldn't be able to grow any food. But I do! I grow all kinds of produce on my tiny balcony.

A few years ago I bought a big plastic Rubbermaid container and I've been growing potatoes in it ever since. Yup! Potatoes! And they're delicious. Pick a new potato, toss it in some boiling water, and I swear it tastes as good as ice cream.

I grow peas and beans on a trellis without much trouble. I've even managed to grow sun-hungry fruits like strawberries and tomatoes even though the people at the garden centre told me there was no way they'd ripen with so little sunshine.

If I can do it, you can do it!

Don't have any outdoor space at all? I have a friend in Northern Canada who grows microgreens on a table by her window. Anything is possible!

12

COOK FROM SCRATCH!

Maybe you already do this. Maybe you were raised in a household where food was love and cooking was an art passed down from one generation to another.

Or maybe you were raised by a microwave and the day you knew you were part of adult society was the day you were finally able to use a can opener by yourself.

Trust me, once you start cooking your own meals and baking from scratch, you'll have no problem dumping processed foods. There are so many delicious meals that really don't take all that long to prepare, and once you get going, unless you're absolutely hopeless in the kitchen, you'll find that the food you prepare yourself tastes way better than the stuff you've been paying the big bucks for in-store.

13

FOODS PREPARED IN-STORE CAN BE PART OF A BALANCED BUDGET!

Okay, I realize this point sounds totally contradictory after the last point advocating for making your own meals from scratch, but here's the thing: foods prepared in-store aren't full of preservatives. That means they can't stay on store shelves for long. And *that* means you can usually get a great deal on fresh foods when the store is clearing them out. Every evening, the shop near me sticks a 50% off sticker on prepared foods you'll want to eat that day. Great for a quick meal, especially if you've got a craving for food cooked by someone else.

14

AVOID INDIVIDUALLY PACKAGED GOODS IN FAVOUR OF BULK PACKAGING.

Not only is it better for the environment, but you're going to save money big-time!

Do you buy those individual servings of oatmeal? Dump 'em. They're full of sugar anyway. It's super-easy to make oatmeal on the stovetop or in the microwave, and when you buy a big bag of oats you're saving money like a pro!

15

FIND A GREAT PRODUCE MARKET TO SAVE BIG MONEY

Fruits and vegetables are so expensive these days!

It's disheartening because I'm sure the high cost of produce in supermarkets means many people aren't consuming enough of these fresh and healthy foods. If you can buy local produce from farmers, perfect. That's the next best thing to growing food yourself.

I buy a lot of my produce from a locally-owned hole-in-the-wall shop where food prices are as low as they get around these parts. This place is not fancy, and all they sell is produce, but it's packed every time I'm in there.

I'd walked past my little market for more than a decade before ever setting foot inside, and when I saw the prices I nearly cried. Finally, I could afford fruits and vegetables! Peppers and strawberries and green beans, whatever's in season. That tiny shop is a godsend.

Take a stroll around your neighbourhood to see if you've got an equivalent you've managed to overlook.

16

SHOP WITH A CALCULATOR TO KEEP TRACK OF WHAT YOU'RE SPENDING

If math is not your friend and you have trouble adding up the cost of groceries in your head, carry a calculator. Maybe you have one on your phone. Don't be afraid to use it. Plenty of people do this. There's no reason to be embarrassed, trust me.

If you're good at sticking to your shopping list and you know in advance what each item is going to cost (because, for instance, they're all flyer sales), then you can add up the cost on paper before you even leave the house.

There's nothing worse than getting to the cash, seeing your total, and your jaw just dropping in shock because *how did the cost of food add up so quickly*?

17

IT'S BETTER TO SHOP ALONE.

Family members (kids in particular) can put pressure on you to buy treats and other items that are way up there on the expensive-o-metre. Go it alone and you won't be tempted to give in to pressure!

18

FAMILIARIZE YOURSELF WITH STORE LAYOUTS.

If you shop at the same supermarket all the time, try to really familiarize yourself with every inch of that place. You'll be amazed what you find hiding in the weirdest places.

There's one supermarket I'd been shopping at for years before I discovered that they "hid" their clearance frozen items in the same refrigerator space as the gluten-free products. I never shop for gluten-free frozen foods, so I'd never had any reason to glance in that direction.

One day I was kind of stuck there waiting for another customer to pass by when I noticed that the bottom few racks in that freezer space had a bunch of random frozen foods shoved in there. Like a stuffed Tofurkey for 74 cents. Tofurkey wasn't on my list, but for 74 cents, what the hay! I'll take two!

From then on, I knew that, whenever staff wasn't sure where to shove frozen items that were on mega-clearance, they threw them in that space under the gluten-free stuff.

As I paid more attention to the store layout, I found other hidey-holes of clearance merchandise. And then I started finding these hidey-holes in other locations, in other stores!

It might be worth asking people on staff for the inside scoop on where to find the best clearance merch.

19

BAKERY CLEARANCE RACKS.

I don't eat a lot of bread, so most of the bakery products that come into my house go directly into the freezer anyway. That's why I don't mind buying day-old bakery products at a discount price.

Sometimes the bakery items you find there aren't even "old," it's just a time of day thing. There's a store near me that clears out all their "fancy" (i.e. expensive) breads in the evening because they'll only sell those breads the day they were baked.

Another supermarket prepares delicious donuts in-store. Around 7 in the evening, they box up what's left and sell them 6 for $1. Just in time for after-dinner cravings, if you ask me.

20

PRODUCE CLEARANCE RACKS.

While your best bet for produce is probably still going to be your local farmer's market or produce market, clearance racks can be good for buying soft fruits for jams and other preserves, or perhaps mushy bananas for banana bread.

Just use common sense. I've seen mouldy food on produce clearance racks. Don't buy mouldy cucumbers unless it's for some kind of science experiment. But other times you get a huge discount because an apple is bruised.

Honestly, if it means saving money I will eat a bruised apple all day long. It's not a big deal.

21

GENERAL MERCHANDISE CLEARANCE.

This is a section I've found hidden away in a tremendous number of supermarkets: a section where the store is clearing out items that are not food.

Very often, I've found this section in an alcove or hallway leading toward staff facilities. You can find really useful stuff on these clearance racks for very low prices.

Often it's seasonal merchandise. Once I paid $1 for sunblock that would normally have cost almost $20 simply because it was the end of summer and the store needed that shelf space for Halloween candy.

On another occasion, I picked up packages of canning lids for 24 cents. I was in heaven because I love making preserves and you can never have too many lids.

22

LOOK UP. LOOK WAAAAY UP! (AND ALSO DOWN!)

Did you know that less expensive items are often stocked on the highest and lowest shelves?

It's true!

That's because people are less likely to look there.

Next time you're buying canned beans or rice or something along those lines, take a look at what's on the highest and lowest shelves. You might just find less costly versions of the items on those prime location middle shelves.

23

NAME BRANDS VERSUS STORE BRANDS

Some foods are worth spending a few extra cents on, but generally things like canned foods aren't discernably different across name brands and generic brands. There comes a point where you know your own tastes, but if you're trying to save money, this is a great place to cut spending. Honestly, to me, canned tomatoes are canned tomatoes are canned tomatoes.

24

MEAT-FREE MONDAYS.

If you're a big meat eater, consider vegetarian options to save money.

You don't have to overhaul your entire life if you don't want to, but consider Meat-free Monday as an option to think about how pricy meat products fit into your weekly meal plan.

One of my favourite meat alternatives is TVP (textured vegetable protein) which can be found at bulk food stores. It costs next to nothing and can be easily rehydrated with hot water. The texture you end up with is something like ground meat. I particularly love TVP in spaghetti sauce for a hearty vegetarian Bolognese.

Another big yum is meatless tacos. I've never had any luck with TVP and tacos, so what I do is sauté some diced onion and red/yellow/orange peppers, then add delicious black beans for protein. This combination goes great with your run-of-the-mill taco mix. When you top it with cheese, lettuce and tomato, to me, that's a tastier taco than the ground beef version.

25

BUY CHOCOLATE ON FEBRUARY 15TH. BUY CANDY CANES ON DECEMBER 26TH.

Buy Halloween candy on November 1st. You get the gist: buy seasonal items after the holidays and you'll usually save 50% or more.

Just be aware that the original prices for most seasonal items were inflated beyond belief in the first place, so only buy this stuff if the price is right.

One year a store near me was clearing out gingerbread house kits for 44 cents after Christmas. For gingerbread, icing and a variety of candies, that was an incredible deal! I spent New Year's Eve that year building and decorating that gingerbread house with my family.

What a cheap date, huh? But it was great fun and it tasted pretty darn good, too.

26

IF IT'S IN THE CHECKOUT AISLE, IT'S OVERPRICED AND YOU PROBABLY DON'T NEED IT ANYWAY.

...unless you came in to buy gum and a pamphlet called *What Your Cat's Astrological Sign Says About You.*

And even if you did come in for gum, you'll get a better deal if you search it out in the candy aisle and buy a multi-pack instead.

If you're looking to save money, any food in the checkout aisle is not for you!

27

SPEAKING OF MULTIPACKS...

Bulk items, family packs and multipacks can certainly save you money, but only if you actually need 100 granola bars and you're going to eat them all before those grains go rancid.

Always check prices on both the individual items and the multipack versions before buying. If you don't pay attention, you can end up paying more for a multipack when you're trying to pay less. That's especially true if a smaller pack is on sale that week.

Always check all product sizes to see which is the better deal. A lot of stores have the price per unit of weight listed on the rack ticket. Have a look to make sure you're not overpaying.

28

DO IT YOURSELF.

There are tons of products, like household cleaners and personal hygiene products, that you can make on the cheap. I use baking soda to clean pretty much everything. It's so much cheaper that household cleaners and a lot less chemically.

29

THAT ITEM YOU CAN'T LIVE WITHOUT? MAYBE YOU CAN!

I used to think I couldn't live without coffee.

Not just that, but I was a bit of a snob about which coffee I bought. I liked a brand that cost a pretty penny, and I made sacrifices in other areas so that I could afford it.

And then I started having heart palpations.

This condition scared me so much that I cut out coffee cold-turkey, something I never imagined I'd be able to do.

If you'd told me to cut out coffee to save money I'd probably have kicked you in the shins, but because it was for health reasons I had no trouble doing it—with the added bonus that I save a bundle every month!

Maybe you can trick yourself into cutting out a guilty pleasure. Tell yourself it's for the good of your body, and it'll also be good for your pocketbook!

30

CHECK THOSE "BEST BEFORE" DATES BEFORE STOCKING UP.

You don't want to buy a bunch of items only to find that, by the time you get around to eating them, they've all gone bad!

If you find grocery items with great clearance prices, there's a chance the store is clearing them out because they're already past their prime. Of course, there's also a chance they're simply clearing out those food items because they've been discontinued by the manufacturer and the store needs that shelf space for other merchandise.

Check those Best Before dates and decide for yourself!

31

USE IT ALL UP!
EVERY LAST BIT!

Some of my best and most innovative meals happen on those days when I look in my fridge and go: "There's nothing to eat!"

Unless you seriously have nothing in your house but mustard and bread (mustard sandwiches, anyone?), you can probably make a meal out of what you have.

Do it! Do it!

I challenge you to make a meal out of odds and ends. I've done it many times and it's always produced weird and wonderful food combinations.

How does this recommendation save you money?

Well, if you run right out to buy new food, I bet you anything you're going to end up wasting that half an onion, those few veggies, that leftover chicken, and whatever else would have made an incredible whatever's-in-the-fridge meal.

Use it all up to save money and prevent food waste!

32

NO BONES ABOUT IT!

I love the idea of using every part of an animal.

If you eat meat, don't forget the bones! Boil them down and you'll end up with a delicious stock. Once you've got your stock, turn it into an amazing soup. Not only does store-bought stock cost money, but it often contains a lot of salt, MSG, and other stuff you don't necessarily want to be consuming.

Plus, your friends and family will be so impressed when you casually mention that you made your soup completely from scratch, stock and all.

33

SHOP WHEN YOU'RE
NOT HUNGRY.

This is usually one of the first pieces of money-saving advice you hear, but you know what they say: clichés are clichés for a reason.

If you shop when you're craving sweet or salty or anything in between, you're more likely to give in to temptation and buy crap that's bad for your body and out of your price range. Avoid, avoid, avoid!

34

KNOW THYSELF.

Ever seen an episode of Hoarders?

I was raised by a food hoarder. For real. I can't set foot inside my mother's basement because it fills me with rage. She has entire rooms filled with food! She's been collecting non-perishables for decades.

If there's one thing that gets my hackles up, it's wasting food, and my mother buys so much food that there's no way she could ever eat it all—particularly the goods that expired in the 1990s.

You think I'm joking. I'm not joking.

Hoarding of this sort can happen for a variety of psychological reasons, but people who grew up during Depression eras or who were raised in a home environment where food was scarce are probably more prone to it.

If you find yourself stashing cereal boxes in dressers and armoires, you might want to ask yourself why you feel you need to have quite so much food on hand. It's not safe from a public health point of view (unless you really love finding baby mice in your cereal), and it definitely isn't good for your bottom line.

35

STAY HOME.

The easiest way to save money on groceries is just to stay home.

Shopping can be a compulsive behaviour like any other. When we think of shopping addictions, our mind probably go first to clothing or shoes, but compulsive food shopping can be problematic too. Particularly for those who tend toward frugality.

You might not NEED a new pair of pants, but you need food to live. Because we need food, it's easier to give ourselves permission to make food purchases.

There's nothing wrong with buying food, of course. This whole book is devoted to the art of saving money while purchasing groceries. But if you find yourself shopping more often than you need to, or grocery shopping for amusement instead of need, and if those shopping trips are costing you more than your budget has room for, it might be time to scale back.

How you can save money if you're always at the store?

Thanks for reading *How to Save Money on Groceries Without Coupons.*

In this book, I've shared with you what has worked for me to minimize spending on groceries and related items. If you put these 35 points into play, or even if you pick and choose your favourite points to implement into your shopping routine, I'm hoping you'll be able to save money on groceries without using coupons.

If I can minimize spending, so can you!

Happy Saving!
Your friend Maddie

ABOUT THE AUTHOR

Madeleine Mayfair is the curator of

Crazy Cat Stuff:
Oddities and Commodities Inspired by Cats
https://crazycatstuff.wordpress.com,

author of a comedic cat-focused alphabet book
appropriately called *A is for A**hole*,

and editor of the anthology
Cat Tales: Twelve Fabulous Feline Fables.

She's also written a series of e-books called
What Should I Write on this Card?
for all those moments when you can't figure out
what to write on a greeting card.
https://whatshouldiwriteonthiscard.wordpress.com